Wh ... ve to go to school?

FOX EYE
PUBLISHING

Why do I have to go to school?

Because there is so much for you to learn before you grow up.

Why can't my parents and carers teach me everything?

Because you can learn better in a group of children, friends, and teachers.

Why should I listen to my teachers?

Because with their help, you will learn new skills and achieve great things for yourself.

After a while, you and your school friends will develop your own unique set of skills.

Some of you will be very good at Science and Maths ...

... and some of you will be very good at Sports.

Some will be good at Music ...
... or Art ...

... and others will be good at Languages and Writing.

(translation)

Everybody is good at something, and learning from others will help you to have a rewarding and happy life.

Let's find out about going to school.

Turn the page over to discover the answers to these questions.

What if I don't feel well?
What if I get hungry?
Will we still be able to play and have fun?
When will you come back to take me home?

Let's find out about going to school.

The answers are...

We will be working and making your home a nice place to be.

Tell your teacher straight away and they will soon make things better.

Tell your teacher and they will call us to come and get you.

Some schools will give you dinner or we will pack something to eat.

Yes! There are times between lessons when you can play and have fun.

I will soon be back this afternoon, to hear about your exciting school day.

How to use this book

You can read this book with one child or a group of children.

The book can be used to begin a discussion around complex questions such as learning why we have to go to school.

The book is also a reading aid, with enlarged and repeated words to help children to develop their reading skills.

How to read the story

Before beginning the story, ensure that the children you are reading to are relaxed and focused.

Take time to look at the enlarged words and the illustrations, and discuss what this book might be about before reading the story.

New words can be tricky for young children to approach.

Sounding them out first, slowly and repeatedly, can help children to learn the words and become familiar with them.

Did you spot
the Tardigrade
hiding in
this book?

First published in 2023 by Fox Eye Publishing
Unit 31, Vulcan House Business Centre,
Vulcan Road, Leicester, LE5 3EF
www.foxeyepublishing.com

Written and illustrated by Simon Couchman

ISBN 978-1-80445-348-3

A catalogue record for this book is available from the British Library.

Printed in China

Titles in the Series